Transparent Thoughts

The Message of Love and Truth

Eugene Kolda

Transparent Thoughts
The Message of Love and Truth

iUniverse, Inc.
Bloomington

TRANSPARENT THOUGHTS
The Message of Love and Truth

iUniverse books may be ordered through booksellers or by contacting:

iUniverse
1663 Liberty Drive
Bloomington, IN 47403
www.iuniverse.com
1-800-Authors (1-800-288-4677)

ISBN: 978-1-4502-9416-4 (sc)

Printed in the United States of America

iUniverse rev. date: 02/17/2011

"Transparent Thoughts – The Message of Love and Truth" are expressed as the simplest, most capacious, deepest and personal. Should this collection seem to anybody a collection of truths too obvious, let them remember that realize the obvious is often enough the first step to inner freedom. Perhaps it is worth doing it. Perhaps sometimes it is worth being transparent.

The Author

LOVE

*H*e walked and stood. He shook, he was infuriated. His head spun. Suddenly he smiled, he cried – he understood love again.

*W*e compare love, since we have not matured to absolute feelings.

*T*o feel is not necessary for love, only last and always call for it.

*T*rue love is defenceless; for this reason it is very exposed to suffering.

*L*ove is an indivisible word, that's why nothing can sneak into it.

*O*utside love there are no other arguments.

*L*ove and life – identity.

I feel that there has to be some love bomb on earth.

*I*n the heart there is always a place for love.

I'm alive, because I love.

*M*y heart is full of veritable diamonds that do not cost a thing.

I always want to live, because I always want to love.

*T*rue love has no shades.

*J*ealousy is a defect, even in love.

*D*istrust in love is learned.

The beginning of love has no end.

The pursuit of life is the pursuit of love.

A rich person – is someone rich in love.

No barrier separates people who truly love each other.

One can talk forever only about love.

Animals also love, but without words.

Erotica – longing for the paradise lost.

*I*t's bad when love is sold, it's very bad when bought.

*H*atred – a kind of defence against love.

*A*nd love today still has the power of lightning.

*O*ne can ask for anything in love.

*F*riendship – a substitute for love.

*P*ain and the heart will always find each other.

*T*he heart is so big, that it can hold everything.

*W*hen I love, I love everything.

*S*ex in love is like marrow in the bone.

*T*he silence is loudest when the heart beats.

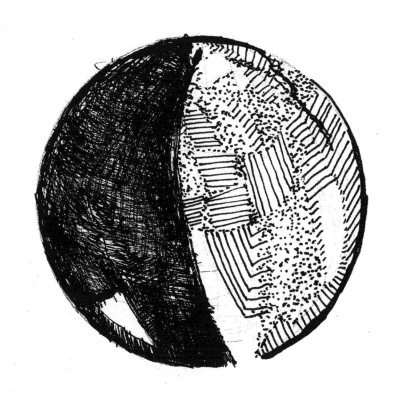

TRUTH

They feasted, drank and danced, praising their wisdom, what the truth is, somehow they didn't decide.

The biggest truths are always the simplest.

Where two truths stand, is one lying?

We have so many truths, but really there is only one.

Truth is never found, it simply is.

The closer to nature, the closer to the truth.

The brain is like a sponge, it absorbs everything.

Ideology – an attempt to shovel an ideal.

*B*e careful with philosophy – it could be different.

*A*nd some sayings can justly be debunked.

*H*idden truths have come out and still more will come, nevertheless the earth cannot come out of orbit.

*S*ooner or later you'll find that truth is exemplary.

*C*riticism – discovering the truth long ago discovered.

*Z*ero - is the only mathematical truth.

*I*nfinity is the only logical parameter.

If a game were found with an unlimited number of variants, the ideal result would be a tie.

Solving the most minor problem reveals the possibility of solving the largest.

To the extent everything has already been said, not much has been remembered.

Turn off the television set for at least a moment, and listen to its inactivity.

After noise silence is once again music.

It's not good when a person suffers for old sins.

We can forgive mistakes sooner when they are committed for us or by us.

If the philosophers didn't think up philosophy, we wouldn't have known what it is, especially that which harms.

Be careful with thought – it is probably the most dangerous matter in the world.

The lack of a response does not eliminate the question.

Conjectures are not yet facts.

Excessive talk does not lose the argument.

*Y*ou can only fathom the entirety when you perceive the detail.

*T*otal freedom – is forgetting it.

*W*e also forget the fact we have forgotten.

*D*evelopment is a path forward and back.

*A*ll matters are normal.

*E*verything that has to take place is not relative, rather unique.

*T*here are no geniuses, since co-authors were born among us.

*T*he best picture is reality.

*T*he worst things said in confiding sound normal.

*E*very ill-considered invention wrecks havoc.

A book, just like television, is different every moment.

*F*or work you have to get enough sleep.

*L*earning – secondary ignorance.

*I*t's not right to conquer your own speed.

*I*deal – a timely value.

*T*oo late means not at all.

*C*rime is not so much a legal problem,
but a medical one.

*T*he best can always be improved.

*O*ne has to undress for deep thought.

*W*e keep on having to learn what has long been
known.

*G*enerally, there is no winner or loser – only a tie.

$\mathcal{I}$t is easier to overcome superstitions than judgments.

$\mathcal{M}$emory lets us down.

$\mathcal{F}$orgetting is an opportunity for everyone.

$\mathcal{W}$hat value is there in still life without living creatures?

$\mathcal{E}$verything is relative, but not for absoluteness.

$\mathcal{Y}$ou turn on the faucet, wash your hands, and turn it off with clean hands, while it is still dirty. So precision slips through your fingers.

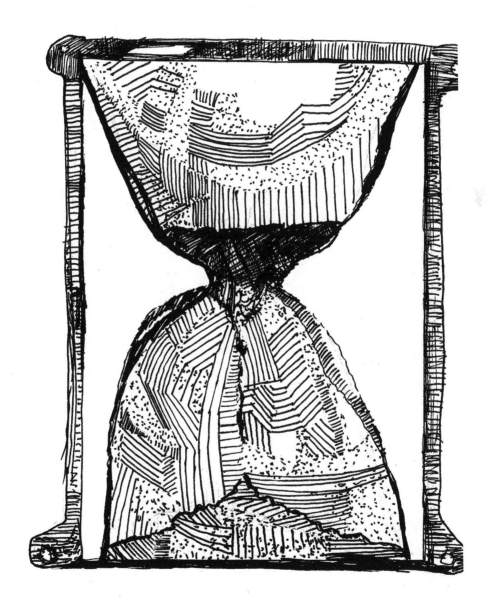

TIME

$\mathcal{T}$ime – made up for life, not for the truth – it is relative. No beginning, no ending. There is no time, there is only being

*W*ithout a beginning and without an end. There is no time, there is continuity.

*L*osing a second in eternity, you lose just this eternity.

*T*here is much time, but what about the time of life?

*T*ake care of the moments, because that much is yours.

*I*n the vast expanse of time, the category of age does not exist.

*T*ime was thought up to make use of life.

*A*t every moment time is just the same.

Reminiscences can also happen now.

The future and the past accumulate "now".

In a given moment you are in one place. For this reason wherever you are, you are everywhere.

Recollection – proof of the present moment.

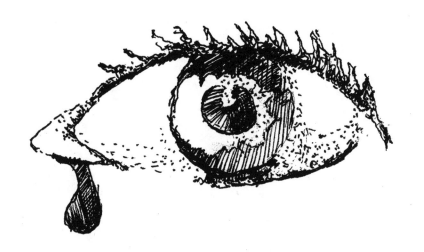

EVIL

Evil gives rise to evil and true wise men will tell you, that it may go around the world, though you might be in misery by then.

The idea of primal evil then gives rise to other kinds.

Through evil, in the twentieth century we came to know all its shades.

It is most difficult to grasp evil in and of itself.

Don't be too good – people tell me. Don't be too bad – I answer them.

Whomever we talk with, everyone complains about evil. It seems that evil people walk only underground.

After the hundredth error you should then admit it.

Don't be afraid to confront evil and it will disappear.

Good or bad – the first choice concerns instincts.

Goodness does not fight with evil, but heals it.

Evil is everything in the mirror of evil, in the mirror of goodness – nothing.

Revenge is continuing a bad start.

Faces cannot be taken and hidden in a pocket.

In the light of evil, one human can compare only to another human.

If you have to be better, then at best be so only for a moment.

Only in suffering does the smallest goodness blossom.

Generally evil does not exist – either something is normal or no.

Evil is a punishment in and of itself.

Only the last shout is the shout of everyone.

Any punishment is also torture.

Everything is relative, but not absoluteness.

Evil and goodness are notions that permit us to lie in the area of moral absurdity.

Careful! Playing with evil means evil.

If even one person suffers because of you, then you're a tyrant.

Just as a huge fire can form from the smallest spark, so from the least evil – the greatest.

A single "no" sounds the bells of goodness.

You'll understand suffering better, feeling it.

All virtues converge into a rainbow.

YOU

*I*f you're on the very bottom, longing to shout, then I'll come running to you, take you in my hands, lift you to a better abyss. Because you still have a heart, though bleeding …
And I'll also be despairing.

I was born and though I could communicate without words, I learned to have a good command of one language, later several others. And in the end I wanted to speak all of them. Afterwards I no longer needed any language.

*H*umans, born in love, yet do not know what life is.

I am human, and for this reason I bind my hopes with people.

*S*uffering, like a person, is no one's property.

*N*o person is alone – there is also the mirror.

*Y*ou don't believe in others, Because others didn't teach you to believe in yourself.

$\mathcal{F}$aith in everything is faith in oneself.

$\mathcal{I}$s marriage possible since everyone is different?

$\mathcal{T}$rue friends are everywhere or nowhere.

$\mathcal{I}$f you claim that people are worth living for, pay attention to yourself as well.

$\mathcal{P}$eople are all the same, only their thoughts are different.

$\mathcal{Y}$ou will understand just how important an individual is when you notice that you are one too.

$\mathcal{T}$o be oneself, means to achieve everything.

A sensitive person first feels, then understands.

*I*f you have no soul, you have no body either.

*A*n idealist is a person who once heard the word ideal.

*W*e feel loneliness only because there are others.

*P*eople who speak sensibly– sing.

*W*here educating individuals or groups is possible, educating everyone is possible too.

*H*umanity comprises a continuous line.

I don't want my own monument, regardless of who I am.

I always see youth in myself.

Even if you were born large, you would have been a child still.

We are born naked and we've also forgotten about this.

You kiss a woman on the hand and you already share her body.

You see someone for the first time and you're happy. What we think counts for so little at the beginning.

They were almost killed because they said: " ... it's human to err" or "…. everything human is close to me".

Posterity is already us.

Since the rich are either unjust or the heirs of such persons, then their poverty is its simple consequence.

Weak by one's own weakness.

Individuals can be mistaken, but not every one.

A human being, this sounds proud.

If you think correctly – you write.

If you're too busy with talk, you can start to think erroneously.

People have an inclination to talk incessantly.

Conversations about people frequently bore people themselves.

Every person has the opportunity to become the biggest monster in the world.

Let's try to educate a single generation.

All senses ideally function simultaneously,

yet thought is not a sense.

Our egoism is cruel.

A good educator should always remember his or her childhood.

A thief notices only thieves.

*B*efore the family arises, two strangers must first meet.

I don't greet or say good-bye to anyone – I simply am.

*T*he king of animals is in fact man.

*T*he best can always be improved.

*P*arents are also mixed in each of us.

*W*e too are sentenced to being with people.

*F*or a outsider, everyone inside is funny.

*W*hen you don't want to be alone, Especially when you're with someone else, then think to yourself that you're with everyone.

LIFE

You will come to believe this, that life is really worth loving.

*L*ife is such a great matter, there is no time for mistakes.

*T*here is only one book – the life of each of us.

*A*ctivities indispensable for life are not work, but life itself.

*E*veryone is born ceremoniously identical and for this reason they are equal.

*B*y virtue of birth everything belongs to everyone.

*Y*ou'll never be short of time to best realize life.

*C*onsent to life takes place without words.

*W*ithout life there is no work, and not the reverse.

*A*nd life is a game anyway – but which one?

*A*nother catastrophe, but this time it still doesn't apply to you.

*W*e are afraid at partings for the reason that we don't know whether they are a final farewell.

*C*igarette – a ritual. The rest as well.

*E*very birth is only another proof of hope.

*I*n travel you are free.

A person condemned by others to death has one more friend – Hope.

*P*aradox: I was condemned due to the fact I'm alive.

*L*ife is a jungle, anyone can be easily killed.

*Y*ou should be care not only how you build, but also how you destroy.

*L*ife itself is a miracle.

I made a mistake, because I forgot again.

*O*ne joke falls to every person.

*L*ife itself is an aphorism.

*W*hen you start to eat only plants as nature intended, all the animals will bow to you.

*S*ometimes a comma decides about life.

*D*eliberations about the meaning of life are its meaning.

*T*oo late means not at all.

*T*he proper division of indivisible excesses – a chance draw.

*W*e have to keep learning what has long been known.

*T*he memory lets us down.

*W*hy hurry through life? Don't we live in an eternal universe?

PEACE

Because evil is also pain, dying or killing And therefore you suffer at this moment You feel this pain or are dying in this pain.

A human person starts every evil, conflict or war.

*C*enturies pass, but the wars are similar.

*W*ars have always existed – only the people and pretexts change.

*S*ince two plus two is four, then why do you kill?

*S*trength is strictly metaphorical.

*I*f peace, then without any weapons.

*T*he smallest injury hurts.

How to reconcile this with the atrocity of war?

Until you stop killing animals, you won't free yourself from the skill of killing.

Systems vary, only the people are the same.

After death enemies immediately become friends.

Every state is the Earth.

Does a friend close the doors to a friend?

Then what are borders for?

A true generalissimus disbands the army and… himself.

*W*hen the weather changes, where will the states touch down on this Earth?

*T*he one who attacks knows no pain; he who has forgotten or doesn't know it is afraid of it.

*F*orgetting is an opportunity for everyone.

*B*orders are transparent anyway.

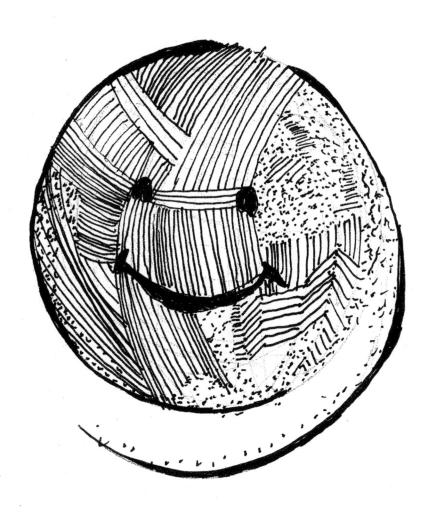

HAPPINESS

The concept of the day, my day: ots of colours, rainbows, joy, and two tears before sleep indeed, due to the easy and close love.

I live everywhere.

*H*ow happy you are. You have the entire universe.

*E*very day should have at least half a holiday.

*A*mong the many colours I can make out a single rainbow.

*I*f I think then I can laugh – I'm already laughing.

*T*he longer you laugh the less you fall sick or the faster you get well.

*F*or a good joke it's worth devoting one's entire life.

And who notices the ugliness and the old age?
The mirror!

Laughter is the greatest majesty of the universe.

I don't greet anyone or say farewell to anyone
– I simply am.

If everyone gave to everyone, everyone would have
something to take.

If things were not toys, then what would we play with.

The more you give the more you receive.

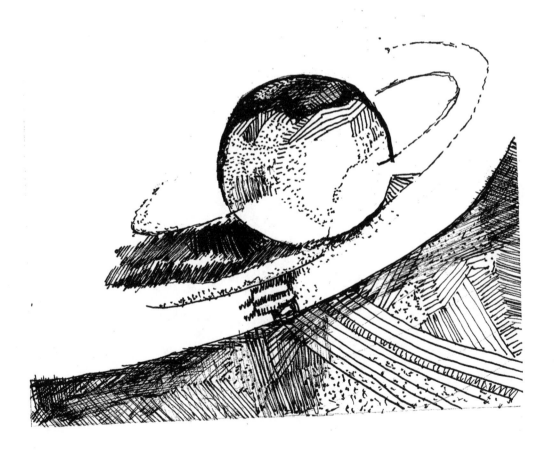

COSMOS

Sweetness in one's mouth, a rainbow in the eyes.
Gardens of nature, senses. Love, The Earth, Universe,
Heaven, You ...

Everything has already been – only the rrangement of atoms changes.

The unfinished universe can also be a form of just a single atom.

In its infinity the universe can be just as huge as it is tiny.

Infinity is too logical to question it.

Calm down. You cannot conquer the universe – It loves you too much, and you're it anyway.

What would the universe be without you?

To speak of anything, you're already speaking of the universe.

*T*hose who sit a bit, strive towards everything impossible in the infinity of the universe.

*L*ook – "Uni-Verse"

*T*he universe has come into life to exclude nothingness.

*T*here would exist no Earth without the help of Cosmos.

*T*he earth would be nothing without all the rights of the universe.

*A*n entity can be formed by the infinity only.

*E*verything that is ideal can only be infinite.

When you cover the space with your eyes, it is like your body covers it too.

Infinity means eternity as well.

You can't really leave the infinity.

Body – vehicle.

Cosmos is infinite because it goes round Love.

You see the sky with your eyes. Some call it universe.

Another name for universe – "0".

Nothing' is also some kind of category.

It is beautiful in every place of the universe.

The only logical parameter is the infinity.

War destroys the universe in you.

If 'nothing' cannot be literal, 'everything' must be.

Question about the universe: If there was only 'nothing', where would be what is?

When time is relative, with no beginning and noending, we see the lack of time to create.

In an infinite universe the beginning can be in any moment.

So many beautiful things happen on the Earth, showing the true Heaven.

So far I have learnt that the Earth is most beautiful.

The nature of the universe is the same everywhere.

The Earth is still on the bottom – together with things beautiful and ugly.

In infinity every place is the same place.

In infinity distance, speed and time do not matter at all.

*T*he Earth – Clean Land.

*U*niverse is you.

END

The rest of the book is also about love, since it is an inexhaustible subject. Therefore, let it tell you the rest...

Contents